ENDANGERED ANIMALS AROUND THE WORLD

ENDANGERED

FISH
AROUND THE WORLD

BY LISA J. AMSTUTZ

PEBBLE
a capstone imprint

Published by Pebble, an imprint of Capstone
1710 Roe Crest Drive, North Mankato, Minnesota 56003
capstonepub.com

Copyright © 2025 by Capstone. All rights reserved. No part of this
publication may be reproduced in whole or in part, or stored in a retrieval
system, or transmitted in any form or by any means, electronic, mechanical,
photocopying, recording, or otherwise, without written permission of the
publisher.

Library of Congress Cataloging-in-Publication Data is available on
the Library of Congress website.

ISBN: 9780756578336 (hardcover)
ISBN: 9780756578541 (paperback)
ISBN: 9780756578558 (ebook PDF)

Summary: From sharks with oddly shaped heads to fish that look like they
have hands, these endangered fish are having a tough time. Learn about
some incredible fish that need our help to survive.

Editorial Credits
Editor: Ericka Smith; Designer: Sarah Bennett; Media Researcher: Svetlana
Zhurkin; Production Specialist: Katy LaVigne

Image Credits
Getty Images: ajcabeza, 27, Alastair Pollock Photography, cover,
Hailshadow, 13, Michel Viard, 17, Natalie Fobes, 24, Rob Atherton, 26,
Sirachai Arunrugstichai, 15, SolStock, 29, Stephen Frink, 9, stevelenzphoto,
25, Universal Images Group/Auscape, 22, Zocha_K, 18; Shutterstock:
asantosg, 7, Drew McArthur, 12, ivSky, 21, Jesus Cobaleda, 23,
Jsegalexplore, 11, OlegDoroshin, 20, Sentelia, 19, Viacheslav Lopatin, 1,
Vlad61, 5, Watchares Hansawek, 6

Any additional websites and resources referenced in this book are not
maintained, authorized, or sponsored by Capstone. All product and
company names are trademarks™ or registered® trademarks of their
respective holders.

Printed and bound in China. 5827

TABLE OF CONTENTS

All About Endangered Fish 4

Giant Manta Ray 8

Great Hammerhead Shark 10

Nassau Grouper 12

European Eel 16

Beluga Sturgeon 18

Red Handfish 22

Making Progress 24

How You Can Help 28

Glossary 30

Read More 31

Internet Sites 31

Index 32

About the Author 32

Words in **bold** are in the glossary.

All About Endangered Fish

What Is a Fish?

Who can breathe underwater? A fish can! A fish's body is perfect for living in water. It can breathe through gills. And it glides through water using its tail and fins.

Water covers about 71 percent of the Earth. So you can find fish all over the world. There are about 34,000 **species** of fish.

5

What Is an Endangered Fish?

Some fish are **endangered**. If too many die, they may go **extinct**.

Why are some fish in danger? Fish need clean water to live. But in many places, their homes are polluted. Chemicals and soil in the water make fish sick. They also harm the plants and animals fish eat. Overfishing can be a problem too.

Where Do Endangered Fish Live?

Endangered fish can be found all over the world. Many are kinds that people hunt.

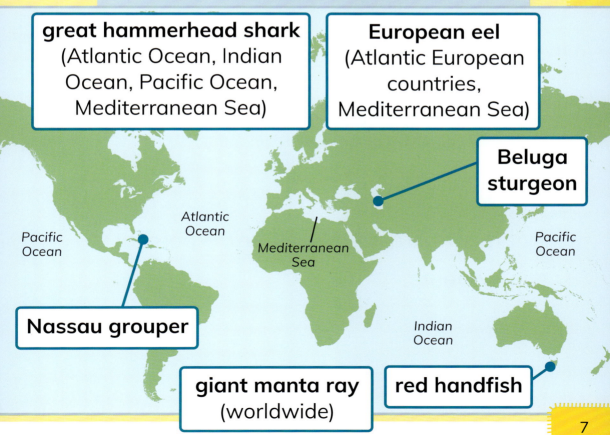

Here's where you can find the fish you'll learn about in this book!

great hammerhead shark (Atlantic Ocean, Indian Ocean, Pacific Ocean, Mediterranean Sea)

European eel (Atlantic European countries, Mediterranean Sea)

Beluga sturgeon

Nassau grouper

giant manta ray (worldwide)

red handfish

Giant Manta Ray

A giant manta ray soars through the water. It looks like a huge bat. Its "wings" can stretch 29 feet (8.8 meters) across. It is the world's largest ray!

Giant manta rays eat **plankton**. But climate change is making food harder to find. Manta rays are hunted for some of their body parts. They also get tangled in fishing nets.

Now, the rays are endangered. Their numbers dropped by 50 to 79 percent in 87 years.

Great Hammerhead Shark

This shark's head looks like a hammer. That comes in handy. It can see prey above and below at the same time.

But that big head can be a problem. It gets easily tangled in fishing nets that catch whatever is in their path.

People overfish great hammerhead sharks too. They make soup from their fins.

Now the shark is endangered in many areas. Its numbers have fallen by 80 percent over the past 70 years.

Nassau Grouper

A speckled fish hides in a coral reef. Its stripes help it blend in. It's a Nassau grouper.

The Nassau grouper can grow to 4 feet (1.2 m) long. It can weigh more than 50 pounds (23 kilograms).

Nassau groupers gather every year to **spawn**. This makes them easy to catch. Too easy! Overfishing is a big problem.

Climate change is a problem too. It harms coral reefs where groupers live. They feed and lay eggs there. They need reefs to survive.

The Nassau grouper is now endangered. Its numbers fell by 60 percent over about 30 years. But some countries now protect it from overfishing.

Coral reefs that died because of warming waters

European Eel

A European eel glides down the river toward the sea. It will spawn there before it dies. In a few years, its young will find their way back home.

But the European eel is in trouble. It must fight parasites and **invasive species**. Dams block its migration. And people catch it to make pies and jellies.

The European eel is one of the world's most endangered fish. Its numbers have dropped by 95 percent in the past 40 years.

Beluga Sturgeon

A Beluga sturgeon lurks deep in the sea. This long-nosed fish can live up to 100 years. Every 4 to 8 years, it swims into rivers to spawn. Then it returns home to the Caspian Sea.

A dam on a river in Russia

Now, most of the rivers are blocked by dams. Fish lifts can help move fish through. But many do not make it. And those that do may not be able to return.

Sturgeon eggs are called **caviar**. People prize them as food. So overfishing is a problem too.

The Beluga sturgeon has become endangered. There are laws against catching them. But **poachers** still kill many Beluga sturgeon.

Red Handfish

This funny fish looks like it's walking on its hands. That's why it's called a handfish. The red handfish lives in one small bay in Tasmania. Only about 100 are left in the wild.

a sea urchin

Habitat loss and pollution are big problems for this small fish. The seaweed that shelters it is dying off. Higher numbers of sea urchins that eat the seaweed are a threat too.

Making Progress

Sockeye Salmon

Sockeye salmon once swam 900 miles (1,448 kilometers) to spawn in Idaho's Snake River. Their young swam back to the ocean to feed.

But dams were built in the 1970s. They blocked the fish's path. The river grew more polluted too. By 1991, very few salmon were left.

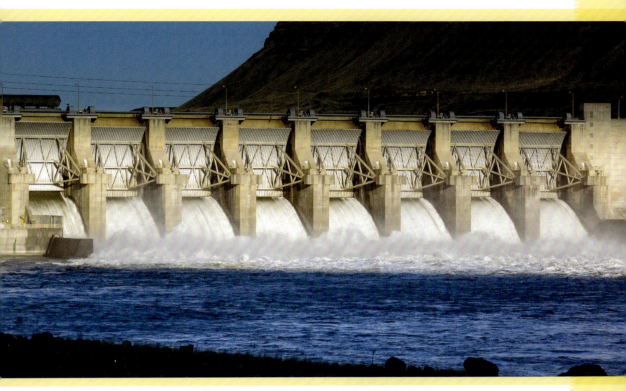

A dam on the Snake River

That's when Indigenous tribes, scientists, and a power company teamed up. They started raising salmon in **hatcheries**. They released some into the wild. Slowly, the fish started to return to the river.

Atlantic Bluefin Tuna

A silver fish charges through a **school** of herring. Its sharp eyes make it a good hunter. This Atlantic bluefin tuna is the size of a boat. It is as heavy as a horse!

People love to eat tuna. They caught too many Atlantic bluefin tuna. Eventually, the fish became endangered.

In 2006, new laws banned planes that help people find tuna. Only fish that meet a minimum size can be caught. Now, their population is growing.

How You Can Help

There are many ways you can help endangered fish, even if you live far from a body of water. Here are some ideas:

» Don't use toxic chemicals at home. These can end up in waterways.

» Help keep waterways clean—don't litter.

» Reduce your use of plastic bags.

» Join a river or beach cleanup.

» Spread the word!

GLOSSARY

caviar (KA-vee-ahr)—the salted eggs of a large fish

endangered (en-DAYN-juhrd)—in danger of dying out

extinct (ek-STINGKT)—no longer living

habitat (HAB-uh-tat)—the natural place and conditions in which a plant or animal lives

hatchery (HACH-er-ee)—a place where fish eggs are allowed to hatch

invasive species (in-VAY-siv SPEE-sheez)—a plant or animal that has been brought to a place where it does not normally live

plankton (PLANGK-tuhn)—tiny plants and animals that float in the sea

poacher (POHCH-ur)—a person who hunts or fishes illegally

school (SKOOL)—a large number of the same kind of fish swimming and feeding together

spawn (SPON)—to lay eggs

species (SPEE-sheez)—a group of animals with similar features

READ MORE

Amstutz, Lisa J. *Endangered Amphibians Around the World*. North Mankato, MN: Capstone, 2025.

Jackson, Carlee. *Sharks: What Do Great Whites, Hammerheads, and Whale Sharks Get Up To All Day?* New York: Neon Squid, 2022.

Stiassny, Melanie. *The Fantastic World of Fish*. United States: Puppy Dogs & Ice Cream, 2021.

INTERNET SITES

Britannica Kids: Endangered Species
kids.britannica.com/kids/article/endangered-species/353099

Kiddle: Endangered Species Facts for Kids
kids.kiddle.co/Endangered_species

National Geographic Kids: Fish
kids.nationalgeographic.com/animals/fish

INDEX

Atlantic bluefin tuna, 26–27

Beluga sturgeon, 7, 18–21

Caspian Sea, 18
caviar, 20
climate change, 8, 14
coral reefs, 12, 14, 15

dams, 16, 19, 24, 25

European eels, 7, 16–17

giant manta rays, 7, 8–9
great hammerhead sharks, 7, 10–11

Idaho, 24

Nassau groupers, 7, 12–15

poachers, 21
pollution, 6, 23, 24

red handfish, 7, 22–23
Russia, 19

sea urchins, 23
seaweed, 23
Snake River, 24, 25
sockeye salmon, 24–25

Tasmania, 22

ABOUT THE AUTHOR

Lisa J. Amstutz is the author of more than 150 children's books. A former outdoor educator, she holds degrees in biology and environmental science. Lisa enjoys learning fun facts about science and sharing them with kids. She lives on a small farm with her family.